W9-BKC-911

McCordsville Elementary
Media Center

FORTVILLE VERNON - TWP PUBLIC LIBRARY
825 EAST BROADWAY
FORTVILLE, IN 46040

DEMCO

A New True Book

KANGAROOS

By Emilie U. Lepthien

CHILDRENS PRESS ®
CHICAGO

FORTVILLE VERNON - TWP PUBLIC LIBRARY
625 EAST BROADWAY
FORTVILLE, IN 46040

Gray kangaroos

PHOTO CREDITS

Auscape—© Jean-Paul Ferrero, 28

© Reinhard Brucker—8, 13 (left)

© Cameramann International, Ltd.—14

H. Armstrong Roberts—© N. Orabona, 21

Odyssey/Chicago—© Robert Frerck, 23, 39 (right), 42

Photri—11

Root Resources—© Anthony Mercieca, 39 (left)

Tom Stack & Associates—© Dave Watts, cover, 2, 16, 20, 25, 36; © John Cancalosi, 24 (right)

Tony Stone Images—© Norbert Wu, 4; © Erik Svenson, 7; © Warren Garst, 24 (left); © Tom & Michelle Grimm, 30; © Michael Townsend, 38 (right)

SuperStock International, Inc.—© J. Baudisch, 35

Valan—© Arthur Strange, 10 (right), 32; © Dr. A. Farquhar, 13 (right), 43; © John Cancalosi, 19, 26, 38 (left), 39 (center), 40, 44-45

Visuals Unlimited—© Joe McDonald, 10 (left); © Carlyn Galati, 17

COVER: Eastern gray kangaroos

Project Editor: Fran Dyra
Design: Margrit Fiddle
Photo Research: Feldman & Associates, Inc.

Library of Congress Cataloging-in-Publication Data

Lepthien, Emilie U. (Emilie Utteg)
  Kangaroos / by Emilie U. Lepthien.
    p.   cm.–(A New true book)
  Includes index.
  ISBN 0-516-01075-1
    1. Kangaroos–Juvenile literature. [1. Kangaroos.]
I. Title.
QL737.M35L46 1995   94-36351
599.2–dc20   CIP
                                        AC

Copyright © 1995 by Childrens Press ®, Inc.
All rights reserved. Published simultaneously in Canada.
Printed in the United States of America.
1 2 3 4 5 6 7 8 9 10 R 04 03 02 01 00 99 98 97 96 95

To the members of
Beta Alpha Chapter,
The Delta Kappa Gamma
Society International

TABLE OF CONTENTS

A STRANGE ANIMAL

When the first Europeans came to Australia more than 200 years ago, they saw a strange sight. Large, furry animals with long, powerful hind legs were hopping across the landscape.

The Europeans asked the aborigines, or native Australians, what kind of animals these were. The aborigines said *kangaroo,*

Opposite page: Kangaroos hop about on their long hind legs.

which means "I don't understand" in their language. But the Europeans thought *kangaroo* was the animal's name—and the name stuck.

Kangaroos are mammals. They are warm-blooded animals. Their young are born alive and feed on their mother's milk.

Kangaroos are also marsupials—animals who raise their young in a pouch on the mother's belly.

There are over 250 species of marsupials.

Baby kangaroos are raised in a pouch on the mother's belly.

Most of them live in Australia and on nearby islands.

Some marsupials live in Central and South America. The opossum is the only marsupial found in North America.

The opossum is a marsupial.

RED AND GRAY KANGAROOS

The scientific name of the kangaroo family is *Macropodidae,* meaning "big-footed." This family has over forty species, but only the large red and gray species are called "kangaroos." Red and gray kangaroos live all over Australia.

Red kangaroos live in the dry grasslands and desertlike areas of

Red kangaroos (left) live in drier, desertlike areas. Gray kangaroos (right) like the wetter grasslands and woods.

Australia. They get their name from the reddish color of the male's fur.

Gray kangaroos are found in the grasslands and forests of eastern and western Australia. They usually have gray coats.

A full-grown buck, or male kangaroo, may weigh up to 170 pounds (77 kilograms) and stand 4 to 5 feet (1.2 to 1.5 meters) tall. Females, called does, are smaller.

Male and female gray kangaroos

POWERFUL FEET AND LEGS

Kangaroos have long, powerful hind legs. There are four toes on each long hind foot.

The big middle toe ends in a sharp, strong nail. The toe on the outside of the foot is smaller. These middle and outer toes are used to help the kangaroo leap far and high.

There are two other toes with curved nails on the

The big middle toe on a kangaroo's hind foot (above) has a long, strong nail. The short front legs (right) have sharp claws on each of five "fingers."

inside of each hind foot:
The animal uses them for
grooming and scratching.

13

The kangaroo's long, thick tail is strong and muscular.

14

TAILS AND TEETH

The kangaroo always walks forward. Its long, muscular tail prevents the kangaroo from backing up.

A kangaroo sits up by stretching its tail out behind it. Its long tail also helps balance the animal when it is leaping.

Sometimes male kangaroos fight among themselves.

Kangaroos are peaceful
animals, but they will fight
if attacked. They balance
on their strong tail and kick
the attacker with their feet.

Red and gray kangaroos spend much time every day grazing.

Kangaroos are herbivores— they eat only plants. Red and gray kangaroos eat mainly grass.

All kangaroos have six upper front teeth and two long lower ones. They use their front teeth for cutting off grasses. There is a space between the front teeth and the twelve back teeth, or molars. The molars are used to grind and chew food.

Kangaroos have extra molars inside their jaws. When a molar wears down from grinding food, it falls out and a new tooth takes its place. A kangaroo can grow about sixteen new teeth for each molar.

Mother and joey eating grass together

Kangaroos can survive on very little water. But they prefer to live in areas where grass, water, and shade are plentiful. They will travel long distances to find the grass and water they need.

GRACEFUL ANIMALS

Kangaroos are graceful when they leap. They hold their short front legs close to their chests. Some kangaroos cross their feet in front.

The tail is held high. It

Kangaroos can hop along at speeds of up to 35 miles (56 kilometers) per hour.

A kangaroo
chasing
butterflies
at the
Los Angeles zoo

works like a rudder to
balance the animal.

When kangaroos hop
slowly, the tail thumps
on the ground each time
they land.

Even when they walk,

kangaroos look graceful.
They start by pushing
themselves forward on
their hind legs. Then they
put down their front legs
and tail. Balancing on
their front legs and tail,
they swing their hind legs
forward. Then they repeat
their leg movement.

In the heat of the day
kangaroos try to find a
shady place to rest.
Sometimes they scratch
away the topsoil to make

a hollow. They like to lie down on their back in the cool soil.

Kangaroos usually lean on one elbow to rest. At times they kick up a cloud of dust to drive the flies away.

A kangaroo resting on its elbow

Dingoes (left) are the main predators of kangaroos besides humans.
Hunters harvest kangaroo meat (right) to feed dogs and people.

PREDATORS

The main predators of kangaroos are humans and dingoes—the wild dogs of Australia. Their good hearing warns kangaroos when an enemy is near. Their large ears are

24

Kangaroos have large ears to help them hear well. Their keen senses of sight and smell also help protect them from enemies.

constantly turning and twitching. Their sense of smell is also sharp, and their keen eyesight helps them see predators a long way off.

Kangaroos use their

25

McCordsville Elementary
Media Center

Kangaroos use their great speed to escape from danger.

speed to escape. They
can hop at speeds of up
to 35 miles (56 kilometers)
per hour. They can cover
up to 20 feet (6 meters) in
a single jump and leap over
6-foot (2-meter) fences.

JOEYS

Young kangaroos are called joeys. About a month after the doe mates, the baby is ready to be born. The doe sits upright and spreads her long hind legs apart in front of her. If there is a tree nearby, she leans against it.

Soon, a tiny, pink, hairless body emerges. About the size of a lima bean, this newborn embryo weighs only a fraction of an ounce.

The embryo grips its mother's fur with the needlelike claws on its front legs. In less than five minutes it travels about 6 inches (15 centimeters) up through her fur and disappears into the pouch.

An eight-week-old embryo clings to a teat in its mother's pouch.

The mother does not help it on its journey.

The embryo is not fully developed. Its hind legs are just tiny buds. A film covers its eyes and ears. It cannot see or hear.

The embryo has two tiny slits for nostrils. It has only a slit for a mouth, but it has no difficulty finding one of its mother's teats, or nipples. Perhaps it can smell the milk. It remains attached to this teat for four months.

LIVING IN THE POUCH

The baby kangaroo grows rapidly. After fifteen weeks the film covering its eyes and ears is gone. Its legs are quite long and its claws are well developed.

But its ears are still small and folded back. And the infant is hairless.

At five months old, a joey will poke its head out of the pouch now and then to eat a little grass.

At six months, the joey is covered with fur and its ears are long and pointed. Now the joey leaves the pouch for short periods of time. But if danger threatens, it dives back inside.

The "young-at-heel" nurses on special high-protein,
high-fat milk until it is over a year old.

THE YOUNG-AT-HEEL

When the joey is about ten months old, the mother kangaroo refuses to let it enter the pouch. She is making room for the new baby that will be born very soon.

However, she still lets the joey nurse. At this stage, the little kangaroo is called a "young-at-heel." Amazingly, the mother kangaroo produces two kinds of milk—a watery milk for its newborns and high-fat, high-protein milk for the young-at-heel.

The young-at-heel stays close to its mother and drinks her milk until it is over a year old. At eighteen months to two years, the young-at-heel will be completely independent.

Opposite page: Mother kangaroo grooming her joey

A mob of kangaroos travel together, grazing and watching for enemies.

THE MOB

Kangaroos travel in a group called a mob. A mob is made up of several females with their joeys and young-at-heels, a large old male called a boomer, and a few young males.

The mob of kangaroos feed together, always on the lookout for predators. When a kangaroo senses danger, it thumps the ground with its hind legs. This warns the rest of the mob, and the animals all take off together.

KANGAROO RELATIVES

Smaller relatives of the red and gray kangaroos include wallabies, wallaroos, rat kangaroos, rock kangaroos, and tree kangaroos.

Wallabies (left) look like red and gray kangaroos, but they are much smaller. Wallaroos (right) live in the hilly regions of Australia.

Tree kangaroos
(far left) like to live in
trees. Rock wallabies (left)
prefer rocky places. The
rat kangaroo (above) is
the smallest member of
the kangaroo family.

Australia is a vast
country with widely varied
landforms and climates.
Each kangaroo species
has its special place.
Some live in trees. Some
prefer cliffs and rocks.
Others like marshes.

39

FORTVILLE - VERNON TWP,
PUBLIC LIBRARY
FORTVILLE, IN 46040

THE FUTURE

Many kangaroos have been killed by humans. Ranchers thought kangaroos were eating grass needed by their flocks of sheep. Other people thought kangaroo meat would make good dog food. It was also used to feed people.

Although many kangaroos live on land that is too poor for agriculture, they still are

41

This sign warns that kangaroos may be crossing the road ahead.

threatened. Part of their natural habitat has been taken over by people. Today, many kangaroos are killed by cars when they cross roads.

Some species of kangaroos have been hunted almost to

extinction. However, they are now protected by law. Every year, a kangaroo census is taken. Officials count the number of kangaroos in each state. The size of the kangaroo population determines how

many of the animals can
be legally hunted.

These protections ensure

the survival of this amazing

animal. Kangaroos will
continue to leap across
Australia and fascinate
everyone who sees them.

WORDS YOU SHOULD KNOW

aborigines (ab • uh • RIJ • ih • neez)—the first people of Australia

census (SEN • siss)—a counting of the number of people or animals in a population

dingo (DING • go)—a wild dog that lives in Australia

embryo (EM • bree • oh)—an animal in the first stages of growth

extinction (ex • TINK • shun)—the complete dying out of a plant or animal species

fascinate (FASS • ih • nait)—to interest very much

graceful (GRAISS • ful)—moving with ease and smoothness

grooming (GROO • ming)—cleaning and combing the fur

habitat (HAB • ih • tat)—home; a place where an animal can find everything it needs to live

herbivore (HER • bih • vor)—an animal that eats only plants

independent (in • dih • PEN • dint)—able to live on its own without help from parents

joey (JOH • ee)—a baby kangaroo

landscape (LAND • skaip)—natural scenery

Macropodidae (mak • roh • PAH • dih • day)—the scientific name of the kangaroo family

mammal (MAM • il)—one of a group of warm-blooded animals that have hair and nurse their young with mother's milk

marsupial (mar • SOO • pee • il)—a mammal whose young are raised in a pouch on the mother's belly

molars (MOH • lerz)—broad, flat back teeth used for grinding food

predator (PREH • dih • ter)—an animal that hunts other animals for food

protein (PROH • teen)—a substance found in milk, meat, and other foods that supplies "building blocks" for the body

rudder (RUH • der)—a movable finlike structure placed at the rear of a boat to help in steering

scientific name (sy • en • TIH • fik NAYME)–a name, usually from the Latin language, that scientists give to a plant or an animal

species (SPEE • sheez)–a group of related plants or animals that are able to interbreed

survive (ser • VYV)–to last; to remain alive after great danger or trouble

triangular (try • ANG • yoo • ler)–shaped like a triangle, with three corners

wallaby (WAWL • uh • bee)–a small kangaroo

wallaroo (wawl • uh • ROO)–a large kangaroo with reddish-gray fur

weaned (WEEND)–starting to eat solid food instead of mother's milk

INDEX

About the Author

Emilie U. Lepthien received her BA and MS degrees and certificate in school administration from Northwestern University. She taught upper-grade science and social studies, wrote and narrated science programs for the Chicago Public Schools' station WBEZ, and was principal in Chicago, Illinois, for twenty years. She received the American Educator's Medal from Freedoms Foundation.

She is a member of Delta Kappa Gamma Society International, Chicago Principals' Association, Illinois Women's Press Association, National Federation of Press Women, and AAUW.

She has written books in the Enchantment of the World, New True Books, and America the Beautiful series.